CAPTURED
and
Crowned

30 DAYS OF DEVOTIONAL PROMISES
WITH JOURNAL

STELLAR CREATIVE | STELLAR MEDIA

Printed and bound in the United States of America
ISBN 978-1515048817

Formatting and Design I Stellar Creative
www.stellarcreates.com
info@stellarcreates.com
405.796.6080

This devotional is dedicated to my precious friend Lisa, for her example of selfless servanthood, her devotion to God and her endless support while she was with us.
Her example and spirit will always be remembered.
I'm sure her heavenly crown is amazing!
#LisaForever

I must thank my Heavenly Father for the lessons he has allowed me to experience throughout my lifetime which caused this devotional to come to life. His undying love for me and constant pursuit of my heart overwhelms me at times. For that, I am forever grateful.

Thank you to my first teacher, my mother Luvenia "Lu" Williams. For the many times I sat with you as a small child learning to read & write, and compose silly songs. You gave me such a loving foundation. My first and best example of an author thank you for sharing your creative gifts with me.

To my loving husband Charles, who listened to me go on and on about this book and my wild dreams to change the world. I thank you for your patience and stability because it has supported me through this process. You're a keeper. :)

To my ride or die Cousin Yvonne, who is my original BFF and will always be. You're the strongest and bravest woman I know next to Nana. Keep fighting and know that you are loved.

To my Pastor, Dr. Charles Martin, II, I thank you for the years of coaching from the pulpit. Your loving correction, advice and guidance have been a source of growth and spiritual healing in my life.

To Anesha Sharp, for being a true friend and accountability partner during this process, your input has been very valuable and your friendship healing to me.

LaTara Bussey, thanks Coach, for all of your words of advice and wisdom on Kingdom principles for branding. I love how God uses you to bring things to light and make them grow!

Finally, to everyone who has offered words of support, encouragement, prayers - I truly appreciate and thank you from the bottom of my heart. God bless!

Jeremiah 29:11

Introduction

Paula [McDade] has captured the heart of so many people. Her energetic approach to growth and healing is unmatched. This book helps you clearly see yourself in a better place and removes the fears and the setbacks that so many of us face in our pursuit of the best possible life. It is a dream-shaping destiny fulfilling guide that will leave you stronger and more prepared than ever before.

Dr. Charles Martin, II | Founder & CEO
Charles Martin Ministries, Inc.

A Higher Definition of Beauty

The Royal Promise
Proverbs 31:30 | Charm is deceptive, and beauty is fleeting; but a woman who fears the Lord is to be praised.

The Royal Decree
Magazines, movies, television, and billboards are filled with images of what the world defines as beauty. When you think of the internet and the thousands of web images that flash across your computer screen, there is no way we can all agree on a true measure of beauty. As a matter of fact, all of these images can be confusing to someone who is still trying to find their identity. Unless we look at how the Bible defines beauty, we can't understand how to see ourselves the way God sees us.

If you watch reality television, the shows are usually all about the relationships between the actors and how they behave on camera. Whether it is housewives, basketball wives or some other form of female reality star, their on-screen personalities are usually bigger than life. We watch because it is entertaining, and the producers know this very well. Underneath the makeup and designer clothing there is a real person, with a real life, and problems just like you and me.

I wonder how it would feel to be famous for spending your lifetime loving and serving people. What if you lived for God in a way that brought such respect to His name that others were drawn to Christ because of you? When you lift God higher than yourself through your attitude and actions, you become attractive to others. Best of all, they won't even know your beauty secret because it has been around since before the beginning of time. Having a heart for God and his people, now that is a true beauty secret!

Talk to the King
God, I want the type of inner beauty that makes my outer beauty shine through in a different way. Show me how to respect and honor you in everything I do. When I come in contact with others, I pray that they see the beauty of the woman I am becoming and not just my outer appearance. Thank you for teaching me how to be beautiful on a whole different level, higher than the world's definition of beauty.

EXPRESSIONS
From the King's Daughter

Alone Doesn't Have to Mean Lonely

The Royal Promise
Psalm 73: 25-26 | Whom have I in heaven but you? And earth has nothing I desire besides you. My flesh and my heart may fail, but God is the strength of my heart and my portion forever.

The Royal Decree
Loneliness is what happens in your mind, more than in your life. Have you ever been in a crowd of people, and still felt all alone? Some women get caught up in this feeling because we like to take care of others. As long as we are alive, there will be chances for us to try and fill that empty feeling with someone or something other than a relationship with Christ. Some may try shopping it away, others may eat to fill the emptiness. Bad relationship choices are often made because we just want someone to be there to love us and keep us from feeling alone. Why do you think there are so many dating sites with millions of members? They're giving the people what they want, someone to "connect" with.

What if we were like the songwriter in today's scripture? Could you imagine telling God how you need His presence? What if you could forget about getting older one day and losing your strength? If we build our belief on something that will last longer than our bodies, we would be totally at peace. Are you at a place in your life where you haven't figured out how to be happy by yourself? It might be time to start taking a deeper look at your relationship with yourself and with God. That is the only way to be more comfortable in your own skin.

Talk to the King
God, I admit that sometimes I choose other things to fill the empty space instead of coming to you. I want to take a closer look at why I make those choices and begin working to change my behaviors. There are times when I don't feel you near me. Help me to know and understand, that even if I don't feel your physical presence, you are with me all the time. I want you to be the one I turn to before I run to other things or people for comfort and affection.

EXPRESSIONS
From the King's Daughter

Decisions…Decisions!

The Royal Promise
Romans 8:28 | And we know that in all things God works for the good of those who love him, who have been called according to his purpose.

The Royal Decree
Have you ever had to decide between something bad and something worse? Often, life will present us with two choices and both of them may not be very good. I've been there before and it always seemed like I was going to lose something in the end. When you're facing tough decisions, there is no way to know how you will feel once the decision is made. You can't guarantee that everything will turn out rosy in the end. All you can do is trust God and make the decision in faith.

Decisions are really about faith and trust. You need faith to understand that no matter what the outcome, it will work out for your good. How do you jump off a cliff with no parachute? You jump and grow wings on the way down. Just remember that you don't have to make the decision on your own. You have the Holy Spirit to guide you in your decision and his answer is always peace. Follow peace. After you've prayed and asked for direction, make the decision that gives you peace. If you feel a certain hesitation – stop and wait. The peaceful decision wins – hands down.

Trust is the other part of the picture because you will need to trust God completely after you say yes. Once you've given your answer, you must walk away with complete confidence that God has your back. When you put your trust in Him, you are saying that He has permission to handle the details from there. So take a deep breath, hold on tight and take a leap of faith. I know it seems scary, but God has your best in mind. He will catch you on the way down because He is your invisible pair of wings.

Talk to the King | Prayer
Lord, when I am faced with big (or small) decisions, help me to understand that you are there with me. I want to be able to surren**der** and let go once I have given my answer. Thank you for giving me wings on the way down. I know that you love and care for me enough now to allow me to make a permanent mess of my life. Your grace is enough to cover any of my steps so that even if I miss the mark, all is well.

EXPRESSIONS
From the King's Daughter

Got Fear? Use Your Night Light!

The Royal Promise
2 Timothy 1:7 | For the Spirit God gave us does not make us timid, but gives us power, love and self-discipline.

The Royal Decree
If someone you loved was giving you a gift, would you accept it? Of course you would! On the other hand, if someone you hated were giving you that same gift, would you be so eager to accept it? Probably not. Fear is a gift the enemy is offering with lots of strings attached. Every time you give in to the fear he places on you, you are accepting his gift and everything that comes with it.

Fear is the container for everything you don't want to happen in your life. It drains you of energy you could be using to fulfill your purpose. Fear stays around longer than it should and takes more than you wanted to give. When you allow fear to take over, it can rob you of the joy and hope you need to continue living your life. My personal experience with fear taught me a valuable lesson about the power of God's word. I have used it to drive away the enemy and overcome depression and anxiety. I use it as a daily prescription to keep those thoughts away and stay healthy.

When a little child is afraid of the dark, their parent usually turns on a night light to drive away the darkness and calm their fears. They know that the only way that child is going to get to sleep is if they can calm down enough to relax and get sleepy. When fear comes into our hearts, the first thing we need to do is turn on our spiritual night light. God provided it through His word and there are many to choose from. The words "Fear not" are used in the bible over 360 times. This should tell us that we are not to fear anything. No sickness, disease, disaster, man, beast, or anything has power over us when we learn not to be afraid. This is one lesson from childhood that we can hold on to. Learn to use your night light!

Talk to the King | Prayer
God, this step I want to take sounds scary but I am ready. I want to trust you with my circumstance and allow you to turn it into something great. I know that I must release the old in order to receive the new. Thank you for giving me the power and the courage to do what is necessary so that I can move forward in your will for my life.

EXPRESSIONS
From the King's Daughter

Family Matters

The Royal Promise
Galatians 4:4-5 | But when the set time had fully come, God sent his Son, born of a woman, born under the law, to redeem those under the law, that we might receive adoption to sonship.

The Royal Decree
Have you ever felt like an outcast or misfit in certain situations? Some people experience feelings of isolation even when they are with a group of people because they just don't fit in. Maybe you're not a part of the in-crowd or popular people. I understand because I have felt that way too.

As part of our identity in Christ, we get to exchange those feelings for a deeper connection to a worldwide family. This family is all over the globe and comes in many nationalities. God has given us a special place among His family because He loves us and paid a high price for us through His son Jesus. Our adoption into the family includes a whole new identity where our belonging is guaranteed. This doesn't mean we will always be accepted by those who don't know Christ, but it does mean that we will never have to feel disconnected again.

Every single day on this planet, there are hundreds of thousands of people waiting to hear the Gospel. They don't know it yet, because they haven't become aware of their need for a savior. To them, they are just living life as normal and hoping that someone will consider them a "good person". We all know good people who never come to Christ and haven't accepted His forgiveness for their sins. Go and meet some of your brothers and sisters in the community. You'll be surprised to find them in the mall, at the barber shop, in the grocery store because they look just like you and me. You're family now, so don't be rude – introduce yourself!

Talk to the King | Prayer
Father, show me the people I am connected to by adoption into your family so that I can begin to find my place in the family. Thank you for churches where we can meet and learn together. As I go about my daily life, help me to identify with others who know you so that I can form new relationships outside of my tight little circle. I need to see the bigger picture so I can embrace the bigger vision for my life in You.

EXPRESSIONS
From the King's Daughter

Constant Conversation

The Royal Promise
Ephesians 6:18 | And pray in the Spirit on all occasions with all kinds of prayers and requests. With this in mind, be alert and always keep on praying for all the Lord's people.

The Royal Decree
Have you ever tried to force a prayer and felt like it just wasn't going anywhere? Did you ever feel as though God didn't really hear you because you weren't in the proper setting or mood? Allow me to let you off the hook when it comes to this topic. Prayer is not a one-time formal event, it is a constant conversation with God. When you begin to look at it this way, it takes the pressure off of trying to "perform" at prayer time.

Our connection to God is so important that the scripture tells us, "In all your ways acknowledge Him and He will direct your path. (Proverbs 3:6) This is actually a scripture about keeping in tune with God so that He can provide the direction we need to make wise choices and decisions. One way to stay in tune with Him is through prayer. How many times have you gone to make an important decision and said a quick prayer for direction? It would be much easier to make those decisions if we would stay in connection with God at all times. We wouldn't have to feel pressured to try to get a quick answer and the decision could be made in a much more peaceful way.

Prayer is as a simple as having a conversation with God as soon as you open your eyes in the morning. Driving to work or your next appointment is another great opportunity. Throughout your day as you sit at your desk or load boxes you can continue the conversation. What I'm saying is, anytime is a good time to pray. Get in the habit of talking to God on a regular and constant basis, then your prayers will feel less forced and more natural. You'll be much more in tune with God and yourself when you choose to pray this way.

Talk to the King | Prayer
Lord, thank you for teaching me a new way to pray. I want to have a daily, ongoing connection with you. There are times when I don't have time to pray a long prayer, so I need to be sure that we are always communicating so that you can hear my heart. I look forward to our talks and fellowshipping with You.

EXPRESSIONS
From the King's Daughter

Good Grief

The Royal Promise
Revelations 21:4 | He will wipe every tear from their eyes. There will be no more death' or mourning or crying or pain, for the old order of things has passed away."

The Royal Decree
Grief is a normal and natural part of life even though it is unpleasant. If we didn't grieve, we wouldn't be mentally healthy or stable. It's not just about losing a loved one either. Grief can come at the loss of a dream, loss of hope or the loss of anything valuable. Some people grieve over the loss of a pet or a job. When you're in the midst of the process, it doesn't feel healthy or fun. It seems as if the process will go on and on forever.

During times of pain and loss, it helps to remember that the hurt will not continue forever. We have a promise of a brighter day because the seasons of life shift just like the sun rises and sets every day. There are many people who have loved and lost, been given a gift to have it taken away. Yet, they still survived the loss and are living proof of the healing power of prayer and surrender. Letting go may be tough, but it is possible.

Be encouraged by meditating on today's scripture. Although you may be crying or sad due to your loss, you will not always feel that way. One day we won't have to feel the pain of loss anymore, but while we're here; it is a good idea to find someone who can support you in this season. Find a trusted friend or counselor you can share with. Join a grief support group and listen to the stories of others who are dealing with similar losses. There is hope for a brighter tomorrow and you don't have to do it alone. God has placed other people around you. All you have to do is reach out and embrace the help that is available to you. I believe that a brighter tomorrow is just around the corner and soon you'll see it too.

Talk to the King | Prayer
Lord, when I am tempted to give in to grief and pain help me to remember your promise to me. One day you will wipe away ever single tear and life will be joyful for eternity. Until then, I trust that you are going to help me walk through any grief I may be feeling. If I am in denial or unable to identify my pain, I ask that you shine your light on it so that I can begin the healing process. Thank you in advance.

EXPRESSIONS
From the King's Daughter

Hide and Seek with God

The Royal Promise
Psalm 139:8 | If I go up to the heavens, You are there; if I make my bed in the depths, you are there.

The Royal Decree
I spent a lifetime playing hide and seek with God because of trust issues. As a child growing up in an abusive situation, I often saw God as a harsh and uncaring Father figure. I thought he was out to punish me for every little thing I did, said or thought. Those trust issues followed me into adulthood and still linger to this day. While I can honestly say I am much better than I used to be, there are days when God has to try harder than others to regain my trust. If I'm not careful, I can find myself standing in the place of that little girl I used to be, unsure if I can be myself with Him.

You may have trust issues with God or know someone else who does. At the end of the day, He knows us better than we know ourselves, so He isn't offended or surprised at our issues. God's heart is that we would heal from those things and walk away whole. No matter where you go, as the Psalmist says in the devotional scripture, God is there. We can't run far enough or fast enough to escape His all-seeing eye. The good news is, God's eye isn't critical or punishing. He is not trying to catch up to us so that he can punish us. He desires intimate fellowship and time with His children.

Don't allow an event like sickness, an accident or some other tragedy to pull you into the arms of God. Come willingly. Take baby steps toward Him and watch Him take giant leaps toward you. You can trust Him even when you don't feel like trusting. Not only will God not disappoint you, He will fulfill your wildest dreams and exceed your greatest expectations. After all, He's the God of the Universe and He has a reputation to protect…right along with His most prized passion – YOU!

Talk to the King | Prayer
God, help me see you through a healthier lens than the one I used to wear as a child. I know your plans for me are good and not evil. You have a future filled with hope waiting for me. I want to be closer to you without having to learn the hard way. I will lean in to you trusting that you will run toward me so we can fellowship together.

EXPRESSIONS
From the King's Daughter

The Favor in Royalty

The Royal Promise
Esther 2:15 | When the turn came for Esther to go to the king, she asked for nothing other than what Hegai, the king's eunuch who was in charge of the harem, suggested. And Esther won the favor of everyone who saw her.

The Royal Decree
Have you ever wondered what it would be like to live the life of a queen? You would receive the finest treatments and clothes, have servants waiting to fulfill your every command. Esther didn't ask to be a queen, but God had a plan for her life which included a royal position so that her people could be saved. These were the same people from which Jesus would eventually be born.

What if Esther decided that she didn't want to obey her Uncle and take part in the biblical version of "The Bachelor"? She could have decided she wasn't good enough, smart enough or pretty enough to compete with all of the other women. Esther could have got caught up comparing herself to them and decided to stay out of the competition. Instead, she took her place with humility because she knew her assignment was about God's will and not her own.

As a Daughter of The King, your royal position isn't about being better than others. It's not about being treated like a celebrity or having riches and material things. Our royalty is a high calling given to us by God because of our acceptance of His son Jesus. We are given the ability to go places and take opportunities so that God can get the glory and His name be made famous. When we step into our true identity as God's daughters, we have an unlimited amount of heavenly favor that can take us a long way! Step into your true position in the Family. You're in good company and good hands.

Talk to the King | Prayer
Lord I thank you for my position as your daughter and my new identity in Christ. Show me how to walk in it and embrace it with joy. I know that there are so many things in store as I take my seat in the world among people who may not know you. I want to be the Salt and Light that you have created me to be among darkness.

EXPRESSIONS
From the King's Daughter

Do You Talk to Yourself?

The Royal Promise
Matthew 9:21 | She said to herself, "If I only touch his cloak, I will be healed."

The Royal Decree
Self-talk is an important part of your development as a person and your spiritual growth. The things you tell yourself about you are some of the most important words you will ever believe. Some people are natural thinkers. They stay in their heads a lot and think about things more deeply than other people. If your "thinker" is broken, your life will show it. That is why it is so important to meditate on what God thinks about you.

There is a childhood saying that goes: Sticks and stones may break my bones but words will never hurt me. We all know that this is not true. A silly childhood rhyme may sound like fun and games, but words, especially the words you believe about yourself can certainly hurt you. I have witnessed adult women call themselves names and say things that are not true and certainly not loving. This is because the messages they are playing in their heads are negative. A person can spend their entire life playing negative messages about themselves through negative self-talk and not even be aware of it. Women and girls are especially at risk, because most of our messages are about the way we look on the inside and how others feel about us.

The scriptures are full of beautiful and amazing words of love and affirmation about you as his child. You can find words of love, healing, promise, hope and protection in the Word. Every time you open the scriptures, you can land on promise after promise about who you are and how much God cares about you. Choose loving, life-giving words instead of negative self-talk. Reprogram your mental computer and clean out the garbage so that you can wear that crown with confidence. After all, you're the Daughter of The King!

Talk to the King | Prayer
Lord, there are times when the things I say and think about myself are not loving. I want to be filled with positive affirmations about myself instead of negative thoughts. Show me in your word how you love me and what you say about me so that I can embrace my true identity.

EXPRESSIONS

From the King's Daughter

Suited for Success

The Royal Promise
Ephesians 6:11 | Put on the full armor of God, so that you can take your stand against the devil's schemes.

The Royal Decree
How do you stand up when you feel like life is constantly knocking you down? What can you use to shield yourself from the troubles of life? Often it feels like we are getting hit with trouble and stress from every side. We might be dealing with a new situation or working on an old issue that keeps showing it's ugly head. Whatever the case may be, life can throw some curve balls and we must stay ready to keep from getting ready.

The "whole armor of God" is described in detail as: The Helmet of Salvation, The Breastplate of Righteousness, The Belt of Truth, The foot coverings of The Good News of Peace, The Sword of the Spirit and Shield of Faith (Eph. 11:14-17). You may not know all of the details of how this armor works, but you can believe that God created it and it works! The assurance of Salvation keeps us mentally secure, the righteousness that Christ give us means we have no worry of being good enough to belong to God. Our truth comes from the Word of God and therefore no other opinion matters. The good news of Peace causes us to walk boldly in the will of God. The Sword of the Spirit carries all the power we need to destroy the work of the enemy. Our faith shields us from being destroyed by the enemy when he begins to attack.

You've just had a short lesson on how to be "Suited for Success" the biblical way. The world has formulas and systems to offer, but the bible has timely principles which have been proven over many long centuries. All you need to do is apply daily and watch God work in your life to help you overcome and succeed in all of your ways.

Talk to the King | Prayer
Father I thank you for giving me the best type of success plan in your Word. Help me to remember to put it on daily and remember that I am not walking around naked. I have all of the armor I need to protect me from the things that could destroy me. Thank you for my armor and for your protection.

EXPRESSIONS

From the King's Daughter

Body Talk: Temple Worship

The Royal Promise
Psalm 149: 13 | I praise you because I am fearfully and wonderfully made;
your works are wonderful, I know that full well.

The Royal Decree
Do you realize all of the wonderful things that your body can do? In spite
of how you might feel about your body, it is amazing and complex. In
order for you to function on a daily basis, your body has to cooperate. We
often complain about our weight and our features, especially when we
don't feel good about ourselves. Perhaps you were teased as a child about
your looks. I remember one day as an insecure teen girl, I wore sandals to
school, and a boy told me that my toes were ugly. From that day on, I
didn't wear sandals again until I was in my thirties. Because I was being
abused at home, my self-esteem was already shattered. I felt ugly on the
inside, and his words made me feel even worse.

The phrase "fearfully and wonderfully made" has been used in songs,
book titles and sermons worldwide. A dear friend of mine who has passed
away founded The Wonderfully Made Foundation. Her organization
ministers to homeless women and their children, providing them not only
shelter, but support services to help them rebuild their lives. Her heart for
women was that they would see their true worth and value, beyond their
temporary circumstances. What a beautiful mission, to help women see
beyond their physical presence and find their inner beauty. When you feel
beautiful and whole on the inside, your physical circumstances change.

Take the time to work on your inner beauty by looking inside your heart to
see what needs to be polished and dusted. You may be surprised what you
find.

Talk to the King | Prayer
God, forgive me for complaining about the body you have given me. It is a
blessing to be able to walk, talk, breathe and hear. There are so many
people who can't do those things. I want to take a fresh new look at my
body image in a way that honors you. Help me to praise you for each and
every part of me. Also, help me to work on my inner beauty even more
than I do the outside. Thank you for the gift of my physical body.

EXPRESSIONS

From the King's Daughter

Who's Your BFF?

The Royal Promise
Proverbs 27: 17 | As iron sharpens iron, so one man sharpens another.

The Royal Decree
Friends are an important part of our growth and development as people. How many times have you had a friend who saw something in you that you couldn't see yourself? Have you ever had a friend who was responsible for helping you develop into a better person? The people we surround ourselves with often determine how far we go in life.

In the bible, David and Jonathan were close friends who developed such a bond that there was nothing that could come between them. The story of their friendship in I Samuel details how Jonathan loved David more than himself. He protected and warned David on several occasions when his father was out to kill him. It must have been very comforting to David to have someone like that in his corner. We should consider ourselves blessed if we have one friend who shows us this type of loyalty and love.

Friendships don't just happen by accident. It takes time to develop and grow a quality friendship. We risk being disappointed and hurt because people are bound to make mistakes. Not only that, but we will probably disappoint our friends at some point too. It is good to remember that friends are there in the flesh, but a faithful friend who will never leave us is Jesus. He is a friend that sticks closer than a brother (or sister) in this case. God calls us friend as we develop a closer relationship to Him and learn more about His ways. Having a relationship with God, Jesus and the Holy Spirit will make us better friends to those around us.

Talk to the King | Prayer
Lord, thank you for quality friendships. I pray that you will help me to be a better friend to those in my life. Show me how to be faithful, loyal and loving toward them. I want them to be better as a result of our relationship. Also, help me to know what true friendship means and to notice when there are those friendships that are not healthy for me.

EXPRESSIONS
From the King's Daughter

Worthy of Your Call

The Royal Promise
2 Thessalonians 1:11 | With this in mind, we constantly pray for you, that our God may make you worthy of his calling, and that by his power he may bring to fruition your every desire for goodness and your every deed prompted by faith.

The Royal Decree
Human beings are complicated, especially the female kind. We feel a different type of pressure to make ourselves worthy enough to do great things. Often it is because we compare ourselves to others or we have a lack of confidence. Often we forget the fact that God is the one who created us for greatness in the first place. The world says do more, be more, and have more, but God says you're already fully equipped. His love gives you the kind of shine that never fades away because your worth is no longer about you – it's about Him. Nothing in your past, present or future can keep you from your purpose if you remember this truth.

If you rely on your own skills, you won't live up to what people expect from you. After all, we are only human and we often all fall short. On the other hand, we shouldn't draw back and expect God to do everything for us. Our feet should be pointed in the direction of our purpose, so put on your shoes and get to stepping. Don't let your education (or lack of), material things or looks determine your worthiness to shine. Get comfortable with the truth that your worth is determined by your relationship to God and Him alone. Becoming worthy is a free gift that comes with your acceptance of Christ, so embrace your purpose with an open heart. Every Daughter of the King is equipped with a little extra dose of favor. Not only does He call and equip you, God also gives you power! Buckle up, hold on tight, and get ready to enjoy the ride.

Talk to the King
God, I don't always have the confidence or courage to step up and walk in my purpose. Help me to understand that your opinion of me caused you to send your son Jesus on my behalf. His sacrifice was enough to give me a brand new life, filled with purpose. I want to use my life to show others how awesome you are and how they can find their worth in you. Thank you Lord for empowering me to do great things for the Kingdom.

EXPRESSIONS
From the King's Daughter

The Best Instant Shame Remover

The Royal Promise
Isaiah 53: 5 | But he was pierced for our transgressions, he was crushed for our iniquities; the punishment that brought us peace was on him, and by his wounds we are healed.

The Royal Decree
Shame is a dirty word that no one wants to talk about. Every one of us has something we have been ashamed about at one time or another. Whether it was an act done to us, or something we carried out ourselves, the feeling of shame is real. How do you get rid of that feeling? One type of shame comes because of something you believe was wrong, but you had no fault in it. For example, being molested, raped or having a crime committed against you. That act was not something you caused or controlled, but you still felt guilt and shame about it.

Maybe you have done something knowing that it was wrong. An abortion, unwed pregnancy or a lifestyle that you knew was not in God's will may be causing feelings of shame. There is an answer for that too. Many women have experienced these things, but they have never told anyone because were too ashamed to face and admit what happened. I believe that God can't heal what we aren't willing to open up and allow him to see.

The key to forgiving and releasing yourself, lies in the promises made to us in the bible. Jesus took the punishment on the cross that would have been ours. He did it so that we could be set free from guilt and shame. Once we confess our sins and release them to God, we are free to forgive, then walk away. As a Daughter of the King, we can exchange our shameful past for a rich and beautiful future.

Talk to the King
God, I know I have some past hurts and old wounds that need to be healed. I'm ready to come clean with you about these things. Help me to be willing to be open and honest with you and with myself, so that I can fully heal. I want to tell others about what you have done for me and how they can receive the same healing when they are ready.

EXPRESSIONS

From the King's Daughter

Trillion Dollar Exchange – You're Worth it!

The Royal Promise
1 Corinthians 6: 20 | you were bought at a price. Therefore honor God with
your bodies.

The Royal Decree
Imagine being raised by two loving parents in a very wealthy household.
You are given the best of everything and educated in the finest schools.
Your every wish is your parent's command, and there are servants waiting
on you hand and foot. Then one day, they sit you down and tell you that
you're adopted. Sounds like a fairy tale doesn't it? You've probably never
thought of yourself as adopted have you? If you were raised by your
natural parent(s) it probably hasn't crossed your mind. If you have been
adopted, it is one of the most loving things a person can do for a child.

I have some really great news for you! Everyone who accepts and forms a
relationship with Christ is adopted into God's family through that
relationship. If you really knew what that meant, you would be super
excited. That means that every privilege and right given to Jesus belongs
to you too! For starters you gain a new home after leaving earth, and it's
not just any old home. Heaven is a very fancy and beautiful place where
everything is much bolder and brighter than here on earth. There are also
benefits like forgiveness for all of the wrongs you've ever done or will do.
You can receive healing when you're sick, have the ability to gain wealth,
and have doors of opportunity opened to you. All of these things come
with a loving Heavenly Father who is always there to hear your prayers,
even when you don't think He is listening.

Now you know why God is trying to capture your heart. He wants to
crown you as His daughter so that you can receive all of these benefits and
more. Great news huh?!

Talk to the King | Prayer
Father, I want to know what it truly means to be adopted into your family.
It sounds like there is so much to learn about my new position as your
daughter. Help me to understand and receive what you have for me, so
that I can tell others.

EXPRESSIONS

From the King's Daughter

Emotional Takeover

The Royal Promise
James 1: 8 | Such a person is double-minded and unstable in all they do.

The Royal Decree
Have you ever felt like your emotions were all over the place? One moment you're happy and something happens to ruin your good mood. Maybe you have flashbacks from time to time about hurtful things someone has said or done.

Emotions were given to us so that we can experience life to the fullest. Without them, we would be like robots, however; too many mood swings can cause us to miss out on the good things life has to offer. One way to take control is to feed your mind daily with positive and uplifting scriptures. The word is like a vitamin shot for our emotional health.

When you have been through tough times your emotions can get pretty beat up. You might be feeling like you may never feel normal again. I can assure you, with a little bit of work, you can begin to have freedom from roller-coaster emotions. Today's scripture tells us that a person who can't get control of his thoughts and emotions is not very reliable. If you want to take back your emotions, here are three things you can do:

1) Read and meditate a positive, uplifting scripture daily.
2) Surround yourself with positive friends and connections.
3) Pray for healing in your mind and emotions. Trust God to answer your prayer.

Talk to the King | Prayer
God, highlight a scripture every day for me to meditate on so that I can begin the reconstruction process in my mind. Help me to surround myself with positive people who want the same good things in life that I want. I pray for healing in my mind and emotions. I know that you can and will answer my prayer.

EXPRESSIONS
From the King's Daughter

What Good is Worry?

The Royal Promise
Matthew 6:25 | "Therefore I tell you, do not worry about your life, what you will eat or drink; or about your body, what you will wear. Is not life more than food, and the body more than clothes?"

The Royal Decree
There are so many things we could find to worry about on a daily basis. Some of us worry more than others, especially if we have been in situations where all of our needs weren't provided. It is easy to get into a habit of worrying about things when we could just turn them over to God. That may be so much easier said than done, but it is something to think about. Not one scripture tells us to worry more to get our needs met. How do you break a pattern of worry? Try taking these steps to a more worry-free life:

1) Pray as soon as you feel worry creeping in. Don't let the worry swirl around in your head for days before you finally talk to God about it. Find a prayer partner to join you in your new worry free lifestyle. You can pray about things together and make your prayers even more powerful.

2) If you like to write, keep a journal and write about your worries. Getting them out on paper takes them out of your head and makes you feel lighter.

3) Keep a worry jar or a God box. Write down your worry on a slip of paper and place it in the container. Leave it there. When God answers your prayer, remove the worry from the container and throw it away.

Remember, that you are God's priceless treasure. His love for you is so big, he is willing to meet you right where you are. The answer to your prayers may come from an unexpected place. He may give you an idea to solve your problem. However God chooses to do it, you can lay down worry and begin to use that energy for something less stressful.

Talk to the King | Prayer
Lord, I know I worry about unnecessary things at times. Help me to learn how to trust you with things that worry me. Give me a peace in my heart and mind that you will come through.

EXPRESSIONS
From the King's Daughter

Feed Your Dreams, Starve Your Fears

The Royal Promise
Ephesians 3:20 | Now to him who is able to do immeasurably more than all we ask or imagine, according to his power that is at work within us,

The Royal Decree
When you continue to feed your dream the dream will feed you – in reality and in your heart. Are you dreaming BIG, BOLD, AUDACIOUS dreams? I'm talking about the kind of dreams that are so scary that you know it has to come from God. By the time most people become adults, they have stopped dreaming. Often in the daily grind of life, we forget to dream. I want to take you on a journey through your dreams. God is the ultimate dream-giver and He can breathe new life into your dreams. He can also give you dreams that you haven't thought of and instruct you on what to do to bring them to pass. I know, because I'm living proof.

Social media has some pros and cons, but one of the good things about it is that it gives us a glimpse into the lives of people who are living their dreams. We get a chance to peek into the world of those who are doing some amazing things. I don't know about you, but it makes me hungry for more of what God has for me. In order to get to more, we have to feed our dreams with the word and by being connected to good people who can push and motivate us.

God uses the abundance in our lives to attract the attention of those who may not know Him. There may be someone in the world who needs to borrow your faith to get to their dreams. This is why we can't keep the goodness that happens in our lives to ourselves.

Talk to the King
God I thank you for the big, bold dreams you have given me. Help me to rely on you to bring them to pass. I do't want to miss out on anything you have for me, so I'm going to stay right here in your will. I look forward to the bright future you have planned for me.

EXPRESSIONS
From the King's Daughter

What is Worship to a Daughter of the King?

The Royal Promise
John 4:23 | Yet a time is coming and has now come when the true worshipers will worship the Father in the Spirit and in truth, for they are the kind of worshipers the Father seeks.

The Royal Decree
I grew up in the church, and as I grew up, worship became associated with a building and certain acts done inside of the church building. It wasn't until I grew in the knowledge of the things of God that I began to realize that worship is the essence of who we are as believers. It's not something we DO, it's who we ARE! Some would argue that you must be a member of a church to be a true worshipper. No matter what your belief about church membership, the word clearly states that we should worship God in Spirit and in truth.

The heart of God longs for people who not only pay him lip service and show up at a building each week as part of an obligation. He isn't as impressed with our church attendance as we might think. In fact, church assembly is more for us than for Him. It is the place we go to learn the bible and it's principles, to fellowship with other Christians and receive prayer and healing. True worship is common to a Daughter of the King, because she knows that her heart, soul and spirit belong to God. An attitude of worship is more about maintaining a constant connection to God in a way which honors Him in all we do. True worshippers know that God is more interested in our desire to lay down our own motives and give Him our all. It's not about being perfect in our daily lives, but admitting that we aren't perfect and our love for God still remains strong. It also includes seeking opportunities to serve and love others even when they don't deserve it. That is the way we as His daughters worship in Spirit and in truth.

Talk to the King
Father, I want to learn to worship you in my everyday life. Let me make a real heart connection from just attending church on a weekly basis to truly worshipping you every day in my actions, thoughts and motives. Allow me to sense your presence everywhere I go, as I seek to draw closer to you.

EXPRESSIONS
From the King's Daughter

Hand Picked Designer Labeled: That's You!

The Royal Promise
Isaiah 43:1 | But now, this is what the Lord says, he who created you, Jacob, he who formed you, Israel: "Do not fear, for I have redeemed you; I have summoned you by name; you are mine.

The Royal Decree
Labels are everywhere! If you look around, you can find them in places you never thought you'd see them. Unfortunately, people can place labels on other human beings that aren't very kind. Maybe you've found yourself labeled something negative in your life. You probably just accepted the label without knowing how to fight back or reject it. As women, we can often find ways of hurting each other with our words, which can cause emotional and spiritual damage. When you've already experienced so much hurt and pain, it can be tough to recover every time somebody opens a fresh wound.

It may be comforting to know that God labeled you before you were even born. Not only did he know your name, but he also knew everything about your personality, your gifting, and your talents. The best news of all is that he has made a way for everything bad that has ever been done to you to be completely erased. Just like that, with one word – one act, it's all gone! You might be saying, "I don't feel like it's gone." All you need to do is to accept the act of love that Christ did when he went to the cross and died. That act was called Redemption. It means that he cleared the slate and wiped it clean from now until eternity for all of mankind – if they will accept it. That's the key right there…acceptance. Give it a try. Exchange your filthy, dirty labels for God's forgiveness and you get to pick a brand new designer label - Daughter of the King!

Talk to the King | Prayer
God, I have been blindly accepting the labels that have been put on me by other people. Today I want to strip off those labels and begin my new identity in you. Show me what to do and how to accept the free gift of redemption. Like your daughter, I want to learn from your word where to find new labels to identify myself with so that I can continue to grow.

EXPRESSIONS

From the King's Daughter

Laugh Yourself Healthy!

The Royal Promise
Proverbs 17:22 | A cheerful heart is good medicine, but a crushed spirit dries up the bones.

The Royal Decree
Laughter is the best exercise for the soul. It's free and you can get it any time. You don't need a license or a prescription to use it, however it is called medicine. Often we get so busy with life that we forget this free gift which gives us relief and distraction from our daily issues. Not only is it good to laugh, it is good to laugh with others. It can ease the tension in moments of silence or soften the mood when the topic is serious.

Laughter draws us closer to one another because it takes down our walls of defense and makes us open to receive. Have you ever noticed that when you're getting too serious your mind becomes very closed to ideas and solutions? Also, when we are feeling that way, it makes us tired and sluggish. A sad spirit often comes from thinking about too many "heavy things". Laughter give us a mental break so that our hearts can catch up with our heads and we can deal with the situation in front of us.

Here are a few ways to put more laughter in your life: Take frequent laugh breaks throughout your day. Grab a friend and go see a funny movie. Watch a silly cartoon. Have a crazy selfie session or a tickle session with your children. Look at some old pictures of yourself and laugh at how goofy you looked.

When you find ways to include more laughter in your life, you'll feel better, the people around you will notice and you'll be much more effective in your calling.

Talk to the King | Prayer
Lord, show me ways to include more joy and laughter in my life. You promised that you would turn my sorrow into laughter. I'm ready to have more joy and laughter on a regular basis so that I can keep my body and my spirit fit. I want to see your goodness and your sense of humor in my daily life because I know you are a God of joy.

EXPRESSIONS

From the King's Daughter

An Affair of the Heart

The Royal Promise
Psalm 51:10 | Create in me a pure heart, O God, and renew a steadfast
spirit within me.

The Royal Decree
Heart surgery is one of the most serious types of procedures done on the
human body. The surgeon must keep the patient alive on a machine while
he takes the most delicate organ and fixes it to work more efficiently. The
heart is not only one of the most vital organs, it is also one of the
strongest and most powerful organs. It pumps about 2,000 gallons of
blood through the body and beats about 100,000 times daily.

The bible also speaks of the heart in a different way. It is the seat of our
spiritual life and the place where our affections lie. The bible tells us to
"guard our hearts" because out of it flow the issues of life (Proverbs 4:23).
With this type of heart disease your spiritual heart is clouded with all
kinds of things that don't please God. Think of the heart as the receiver in
the radio and the flesh as the speaker. The heart receives the signal and
the flesh broadcasts it out for others to hear and see.

The heart, mind and flesh all working together can bring change in your
life when you give them to God. What you feed your mind, eventually
shows up in your heart and what is in the heart shows up in your behavior.
The word of God is a great prescription for heart disease. Working along
with the Holy Spirit, it can create a healthier heart which in turn can begin
to cause the changes needed in your life for growth and spiritual health.

Talk to the King | Prayer
Lord, I want to give my heart to you so that you can clear out anything
that may be standing in the way of our relationship. Help me to be more
open to heart surgery. I know that you are the only one who can change
my heart and my habits so that I can be more like you.

EXPRESSIONS
From the King's Daughter

What Are You Leaving Behind?

The Royal Promise
Philippians 3:13 | Brothers and sisters, I do not consider myself yet to have taken hold of it. But one thing I do: Forgetting what is behind and straining toward what is ahead,

The Royal Decree
None of us likes to think about leaving things behind but it is a necessary step in moving toward our expected end. When we are faced with the possibility of leaving behind our loved ones who may not be "all in" it is a scary thought. Leaving behind a past filled with pain and hurt doesn't seem like such a bad tradeoff for a brighter future…but if it is the only thing we've known, it can still be a scary thing.

Nobody gets out of this life without some sacrifices. Just like Abraham when he was asked to leave his country, we have many sentimental things back in Egypt. It could be a friendship, or a job, maybe an abusive relationship is what we left behind. Rest assured that whatever your sacrifice it is worth letting go to get to the prize.

A runner must be swift and in order to be swift he has to be light. Traveling light means the baggage has to stay. That old mindset has to fall off…that way of thinking and doing things must be laid down so we can pick up a better way of living. So take that leap of faith and give it to Him now. You won't regret your decision. I promise on the other side is something absolutely amazing!

Talk to the King | Prayer
God, this step I want to take sounds scary but I am ready. I want to trust you with my circumstance and allow you to turn it into something great. I know that I must release the old in order to receive the new. Thank you for giving me the power and the courage to do what is necessary so that I can move forward in your will for my life.

EXPRESSIONS
From the King's Daughter

The Question is Why

The Royal Promise
Luke 8: 17 | For there is nothing hidden that will not be disclosed, and nothing concealed that will not be known or brought out into the open.

The Royal Decree
Have you ever questioned God about something you found hard to understand or accept? I know that I have done it myself and then felt guilty for asking. There are times when it is just so hard to accept something that seems wrong or unfair. Even though we know that bad things happen to good people, it is still something that causes confusion in our hearts and minds.

Questioning God is something Job had to wrestle with in the bible. He could not understand why God allowed him to go through such hard things in his life. Job lost his family, home and property. He also lost his health and all of his friends began to turn on him. The one thing he never lost through all of it was his relationship with God. He may have wanted to turn his back on God, but he didn't. Job knew that if God had been good to him before in his life, He would do it again.

When you're tempted to be angry at God for the bad things that have happened, remember that He is not punishing you. God isn't mad at you or trying to get back at you for something in your past. He is a loving God who only wants the best for His children. That's the kind of Father you have, and He is waiting to embrace you even when you question why.

Talk to the King | Prayer
God, there have been things in my life that I didn't understand. I admit that there are times when I've even been angry with you. Help me to feel and understand that you are not punishing me or angry. Your ways are much higher than my ways, so I will trust that you know what is best and have my best interest in mind at all times.

EXPRESSIONS
From the King's Daughter

Future Fear

The Royal Promise
Matthew 6:34 | Therefore do not worry about tomorrow, for tomorrow will worry about itself. Each day has enough trouble of its own.

The Royal Decree
Those of us who have endured any kind of trauma or grief know that it is very easy slip away from being "in the moment" because of worry or fear. Sometimes your mind will just take you away from a nice, peaceful moment to start worrying about the future. No matter what is on your mind, it does no good to worry about it.

When I was a child, I had such a nagging sense of fear about the end of the world. I would literally sit out on my front porch and wait for the stars to begin falling from the sky. One day as I was waiting for doom and destruction to happen to my world, it dawned on me that there was absolutely nothing I could do to stop it from happening. If the end of the world were about to take place, I would be powerless to stop it. It sounds silly to think back about an old childhood fear, but mental habits like fear, worry and dread can follow you into adulthood. Later in life I began to experience anxiety and panic attacks because I had trained my mind to latch on to stressful things and worry about them over and over again. That habit causes the body to produce signals which tell you it's time to fight or flee. If you can't do either, you experience panic and it's not fun.

The word tells us not to worry about tomorrow because it will take care of itself. Our focus should be on the goodness of our Father and how we can get closer to Him so that our fears seem tiny and He becomes bigger in our lives!

Talk to the King
Father, there are times when I let myself worry or silly or small things. I know that if I let go of those things and turn them over to you, you can handle them far better than I ever could. Please show me how to let go and allow you to be the protector I've always needed in my life. Help me forgive those who may not have protected me the way I needed them to.

EXPRESSIONS
From the King's Daughter

Your Secret Is Safe

The Royal Promise
Ecclesiastes 12:14 | For God will bring every deed into judgment, including every hidden thing, whether it is good or evil.

The Royal Decree
Secrets are like poison. They are toxic to your body and mind, waiting to choke the life out of your spirit and make you unable to function in your true calling. I know because I lived with a terrible secret for most of my childhood. I was being molested by a family member and told never to tell another soul or they would be harmed. At the time, I as a young child and I believed this person, so I kept the secret to myself. Although I can share my secret shame with others, there were many years when I was silent and angry.

God promises something very powerful in the word regarding secrets. One day He will judge each and every one of the things done on earth whether good or bad. This promise means that we never have the burden of trying to become judge and jury for another person's actions. Although we don't agree with the wrongs done to us, we can let the person live without our constant judgement of them as a person. The key to our freedom comes in acknowledging the wrong, experiencing the feelings, then forgiving the person who harmed us. It may not be as easy as 1-2-3, but the process will allow you to move on and begin to heal. There may be starts and stops in your journey, but you will soon find that every step becomes lighter and every moment gets easier. Trust God with your secret, then ask him to show you, one other person, you can trust to share it with. By allowing yourself to feel and trust, the secret can no longer hold you hostage.

Talk to the King | Prayer
Lord, all of us have been hurt in some way by another person whether they meant it or not. I ask you to show me the areas where I have been hurt and I'm still holding unforgiveness. I don't want to be bitter or angry anymore. Take my heart and heal it as I release it to your care. Show me how to love myself enough to be open and trusting again.

EXPRESSIONS
From the King's Daughter

Raise the Praise

The Royal Promise
Psalm 148: 5 | Let them praise the name of the LORD, for he commanded and they were created.

The Royal Decree
Praise is what we were created for, just as a pencil is created to write or a crayon to color. Although we have different expressions of praise, we have the same ability to give God praise. As a matter of fact, our forever life will be spent praising him along with the angels.

Have you ever watched a new baby duck as they waddle around learning how to walk on their little webbed feet. At first, it is very shaky but eventually the new duckling is walking like a pro because ducks were created that way. Those same feet allow them to swim on top of the water with ease because they are made like little paddles which help them glide around with ease. Your praise skills may be shaky at first, but as you continue to come into his presence with a sincere heart, praise will become like a second language.

You may not always feel like praising God for everything. Some days it might even be a struggle to find something good to thank and praise him for. If you just start with the small things like waking up in the morning, having food and shelter, that's a good starting place. Take it one step further and share your gratitude with someone else. As you think about the goodness of God in your life, you might just start a praise party that could raise the roof because praise is contagious.

Talk to the King | Prayer
God, I don't always feel like praising, and some days are easier than others. Help me to see that praise is where you live and if I want to be close to you, all I have to do is open my mouth. Thank you for blessing me in so many amazing ways.

EXPRESSIONS
From the King's Daughter

How Do You Forgive the BIG Stuff?

The Royal Promise
Luke 23:34 | Jesus said, "Father, forgive them, for they do not know what they are doing." And they divided up his clothes by casting lots.

The Royal Decree
This scripture is the perfect picture of forgiveness under what seems like an impossible situation. Jesus is hanging on a jagged, wooden cross about to die for the sins of people who don't even accept him. He was made fun of for living out his purpose in life, always being threatened and made fun of, and he is still asking the Father to forgive them. If there was a good example of forgiving the big stuff, this is one example for us to take a close look at.

It isn't easy when you have lost someone or something special. When you've been through a very tough time in your life, it is hard to forgive the people who caused you pain. The grief and sorrow, the anger and rage can feel like it will choke you out. You may even be mad at God for letting you go through such horrible pain and not doing anything to stop it. God knew just how you would feel when His only son was hanging on the cross dying. He had to stand by and watch while he held back from destroying man for their hateful behavior. God did this so that He could save our lives from punishment forever. If Christ could pray for forgiveness for those mean and hateful things, so can you. It may not be easy so to forgive the person who hurt you, left you, scarred or betrayed you. I can tell you that God covers the BIG and the small things. He's waiting for you to reach out to Him so that He can help you forgive one step at a time.

Talk to the King
God, I have some things that we need to talk about so that I can be ready to forgive. I've been hurt in a way that is very deep. I also have some small things that I've been holding on to for too long. I'm coming to you to ask for your help, your guidance, and your direction so that I can learn how to forgive. Show me how and help me to make it a lifestyle.

Father Knows Best

The Royal Promise
Psalm 9:10 | Those who know your name will trust in you, for you, LORD, have never forsaken those who seek you.

The Royal Decree
As a young girl growing up without my father, I felt confused and abandoned. Of course, when you're a child, you don't understand what abandonment really is. I blamed myself for his absence and tried to understand why he didn't love me enough to stick around. I was also being sexually abused by a family member, and the shame ate away at what remained of my self-esteem. All of those negative feelings eventually led me to seek out unhealthy relationships with men to soothe the ache. Teenaged parenthood was the result, and I repeated the cycle twice before I reached the age of 20.

Many women can relate to what I felt. The circumstances may not have been exactly the same, but the feelings usually look very similar. When a father is absent, a trusted male role model can step in to fulfill that role so that she is able to develop a healthy viewpoint of male/female dynamics.

As I began to seek healing from my past, God began to share with me about he sees me as the "apple of his eye" (Psalm 17:8) and how I was "fearfully and wonderfully made" (Psalm 139:14). It took a while for all of this to really soak in, but eventually I starting trusting God little by little. Our relationship began to grow more and more as I allowed him to look into my heart and clear away the hurt, shame and pain I suffered. I can finally say I have a father – one that will never abandon me. One day, we will get to spend all of our time together forever, and that is a wonderful feeling.

Talk to the King | Prayer
God, teach me how to trust again. There are times when I feel like I am all alone and I just need the loving arms of a father. I want to crawl up into your arms and be held until I start to finally exhale. Walk through my dark times with me and guide the way. I want to learn what it feels like to have a beautiful father/daughter relationship the way you intended. Show me in your word what you really think and feel for me.

EXPRESSIONS
From the King's Daughter

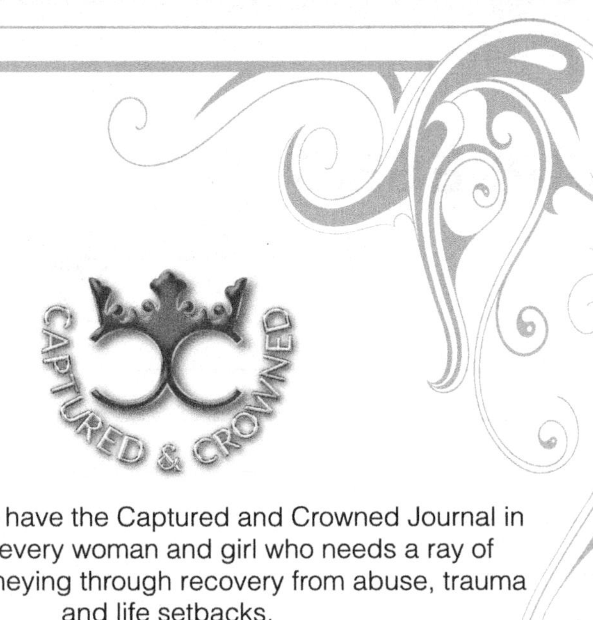

It is our hope to have the Captured and Crowned Journal in the hands of every woman and girl who needs a ray of hope while journeying through recovery from abuse, trauma and life setbacks.

The 7-Day version of this devotional can be downloaded using the YouVersion app to your smartphone, tablet or computer by visiting:
YouVersion.com - search for "Captured and Crowned" under plans.

To learn more about Captured and Crowned, and how you can put a copy of this book into the hands of women and girls who need these devotionals, please visit:

www.capturedandcrowned.org
Email: info@capturedandcrowned.org

We thank you for your ongoing support and prayers.

Paula McDade
Creator & Founder
Captured and Crowned

Made in the USA
Monee, IL
07 July 2026

56552683R00039